MICHAEL J. FOX

A Real-Life Reader Biography

John Bankston

Mitchell Lane Publishers, Inc.

P.O. Box 619
Bear, Delaware 19701
http://www.mitchelllane.com

Printing   1   2   3   4   5   6   7   8   9

Real-Life Reader Biographies

Paula Abdul	Christina Aguilera	Marc Anthony	Lance Armstrong
Drew Barrymore	Tony Blair	Brandy	Garth Brooks
Kobe Bryant	Sandra Bullock	Mariah Carey	Aaron Carter
Cesar Chavez	Roberto Clemente	Christopher Paul Curtis	Roald Dahl
Oscar De La Hoya	Trent Dimas	Celine Dion	Sheila E.
Gloria Estefan	Mary Joe Fernandez	**Michael J. Fox**	Andres Galarraga
Sarah Michelle Gellar	Jeff Gordon	Virginia Hamilton	Mia Hamm
Melissa Joan Hart	Salma Hayek	Jennifer Love Hewitt	Faith Hill
Hollywood Hogan	Katie Holmes	Enrique Iglesias	Allen Iverson
Janet Jackson	Derek Jeter	Steve Jobs	Alicia Keys
Michelle Kwan	Bruce Lee	Jennifer Lopez	Cheech Marin
Ricky Martin	Mark McGwire	Alyssa Milano	Mandy Moore
Chuck Norris	Tommy Nuñez	Rosie O'Donnell	Mary-Kate and Ashley Olsen
Rafael Palmeiro	Gary Paulsen	Colin Powell	Freddie Prinze, Jr.
Condoleezza Rice	Julia Roberts	Robert Rodriguez	J.K. Rowling
Keri Russell	Winona Ryder	Cristina Saralegui	Charles Schulz
Arnold Schwarzenegger	Selena	Maurice Sendak	Dr. Seuss
Shakira	Alicia Silverstone	Jessica Simpson	Sinbad
Jimmy Smits	Sammy Sosa	Britney Spears	Julia Stiles
Ben Stiller	Sheryl Swoopes	Shania Twain	Liv Tyler
Robin Williams	Vanessa Williams	Venus Williams	Tiger Woods

Library of Congress Cataloging-in-Publication Data
Bankston, John, 1974-
    Michael J. Fox : a real-life reader biography / John Bankston.
        p. cm.
    Includes index.
    ISBN 1-58415-128-5 (lib.)
    1. Fox, Michael J., 1961—Juvenile literature. 2. Actors—Canada—Biography—Juvenile literature. 3. Actors—United States—Biography—Juvenile literature. I. Title.
    PN2308.F69 B36 2002
    791.43′028′092—dc21
    [B]

20020254

ABOUT THE AUTHOR: Born in Boston, Massachussetts, **John Bankston** began publishing articles in newspapers and magazines while still a teenager. Since then, he has written over two hundred articles, and contributed chapters to books such as *Crimes of Passion*, and *Death Row 2000*, which have been sold in bookstores across the world. He currently lives in Los Angeles, California, pursuing a career in the entertainment industry.
PHOTO CREDITS: Cover: Dreamworks/Getty Images; p. 4 Yoram Kahana/Shooting Star; p. 6 John Barrett/Globe Photo p. 9 George De Sota/Getty Image; p. 12 Neal Preston/Corbis; p. 14 The Kobal Collection; p. 19 Universal Pictures/Getty Images; p. 22 Tom Rodriguez/Globe Photos; p. 26 AP; p. 29 Dreamworks/Getty Images
ACKNOWLEDGMENTS: The following story has been thoroughly researched, and to the best of our knowledge, represents a true story. While every possible effort has been made to ensure accuracy, the publisher will not assume liability for damages caused by inaccuracies in the data, and makes no warranty on the accuracy of the information contained herein. This story has not been authorized nor endorsed by Michael J. Fox.

Table of Contents

Chapter 1
Changing Dreams

Growing up in Canada, many young boys dream of becoming hockey players. It is a normal ambition in a country where the game is played by groups of kids as often as pick up games of basketball and football are played in the United States. Michael Fox loved hockey and dreamed of a career where there were no rules – a job unlike those done by his parents or their friends. "I had all the usual ambition growing up," Michael later admitted to the *Port Arthur News*. "I wanted to be a writer, a musician, a hockey player. I wanted to do something that wasn't nine to five."

Michael Fox loved hockey and dreamed of a career where there were no rules.

Michael J. Fox gave up on his dream of being a hockey player because of his height.

There was only one problem. By the time he was 15, Michael still was less than five feet tall. Hockey was out of the question. Fortunately, there were other dreams.

Michael Andrew Fox was born on June 9, 1961 to Bill and Phyllis Fox in the town of Edmonton, part of the Canadian province of Alberta. His father had been in the Canadian Army, before serving in the Edmonton Police for 15 years. During his childhood, the Fox family moved often. Michael was always the new kid. He was also small. The only way he could keep from getting picked on was to be funny. Luckily, he was good at it.

Keeping others entertained was a natural gift. At home, in addition to his parents, there were four other kids - Karen, Steve, Jacki and Kelli. Michael had to be pretty sharp to keep their attention. "The oldest form of theater is the dinner table," Michael told *Rolling Stone Magazine.* "It's got five or six people, a new show every night." Between school and home, Michael was able to develop a natural comedic talent.

By the time he arrived in Burnaby, a suburb of Vancouver, British Columbia, Michael was already good at making jokes and winning new friends. He was also quickly realizing how unrealistic his dreams of being a pro hockey player were.

Michael was great on the ice - he had good speed and energy. He was also one of the shortest players on the team, and while the others were growing, it began to look like he would never grow taller than five feet. He developed other interests by playing guitar in a band and acting in high school.

Vancouver was a great place for an aspiring actor like Michael to live. Toronto and Vancouver are both prime locations for

Keeping others entertained was a natural gift for Michael.

Canadian film production. Like New York and Los Angeles in the United States, these two Canadian cities draw actors and film crews from around the world.

At 15, Michael got his big break. He also discovered one way being small for his age could be an advantage. He had been taking drama classes at school for some time when his teacher, Ross Jones, learned the Canadian Broadcasting Corporation was holding auditions for a pilot–a tryout TV show.

Michael went to the audition for *Leo and Me*. At first, casting directors—the people in charge of auditioning actors—were not sure they wanted to even see Michael. The role was for a kid under the age of 12. Michael was 16. Then they met him. "When he came in, I swear the air changed," casting director Heather Jones admitted in Canadian newspaper *The Toronto Globe and Mail.*

Michael got the part. Under the name "Mike Fox," he played the orphaned nephew of a rich single man who was forced to raise him. The show aired in October of 1978, but the show's producers soon had a problem.

Michael Fox was growing.

The show only lasted 12 episodes, but by the time it was over, Michael's voice had changed, he had lost his baby fat, and he had grown several inches. Although just over five feet tall, Michael hoped the growth spurt would continue.

After the TV show went off the air, he won his first part in a professional play, *The Shadow Box*. This time he played a 14-year-old. He landed more and more acting work, but his grades suffered as he took off time from school. He had always done well in school before, but by his senior year, Michael was even failing drama.

Michael with his mother Phyllis

After winning a part in the Paramount TV movie, *Letters from Frank*, he left for filming in Los Angeles. His parents were played by veteran actors Maureen Stapleton and Art Carney. The two both saw something promising in the young man, and told him he should pursue his dreams of becoming a professional actor.

Michael did not waste any time.

He dropped out of high school and moved to Los Angeles. His parents were very concerned; most high school dropouts do not become successful.

However, they might have taken comfort in the words of Michael's grandmother who often said, "Don't worry, he'll get through it and then he'll be famous someday."

Chapter 2
The Perfect Thermos

Becoming a working actor in Los Angeles is never easy, but for the Canadian-born Michael it was even more difficult. While most struggling actors are able to supplement their income with "day jobs"—working in restaurants or offices— as a foreign worker, Michael was only allowed to work as an actor.

In the beginning, Michael had an easier time of it than most. Already a member of the actor's union—the Screen Actor's Guild—Michael added the "J" to his name when he learned an actor on a soap opera named Michael Fox was already in the union. Instead of his own middle initial, he decided to use the initial

As a foreign worker, Michael was not allowed to supplement his income with a day job.

Michael performs at Comic Relief in 1987.

"J" in honor of character actor Michael "J" Pollard.

With connections from his work on *Letters from Frank*, he was quickly cast in Disney's *Midnight Madness*. The attempt by Disney to make an adult-oriented film failed to make any money. Michael's next film, *Class of 1984*, a movie about tough kids, was not much of a success either.

Although Michael had supplemented his income with guest spots on TV shows and a short-lived series, *Palmerstown, USA,* after *Class of 1984*, his phone stopped ringing.

At first it stopped ringing because his agent did not have any auditions for him to go to. Then it stopped ringing because Michael did not pay his bill. There were a lot of unpaid bills for Michael J. Fox in the early 1980s.

Although his work had earned him over $60,000 in a fairly short period of time, Michael spent every penny on a nice apartment, new furniture and an upscale lifestyle.

"I was an idiot," he admitted later in an interview with *Rolling Stone Magazine.* He moved into a garage apartment, using a payphone next to a restaurant to talk to his agent. He sold his sectional couch piece by piece, and lived off of credit cards, until he was $30,000 in debt. Despite the hardship, the struggle had one important advantage.

Los Angeles is a very image-conscious town, and the truth is thin actors usually work more than heavy ones. Although he had stopped growing when he reached 5-foot 4 inches, the meals and goodies available on film and TV sets, along with plenty of gourmet meals, helped balloon his weight to over 140 pounds. Looking so chubby kept him from getting parts.

His new poverty forced him to cut back on his eating, a kind of poor man's diet. It did him a world of good when he auditioned for a new NBC program called *Family Ties.*

Although Michael earned a lot of money in a short period of time, he spent every penny on an apartment, furniture and an upscale lifestyle.

Michael with his Family Ties *castmates*

The show was about former 1960s hippies—people who believed in peace, love, and living outside of "conventional society"—struggling to raise three kids in the 1980s, a decade focused on money.

Unfortunately, Michael blew his first audition. He came across as too arrogant and unlikable. But the casting director saw something in the young man's performance and convinced the show's producer, Gary David Goldberg, to give Michael another chance. Despite

Goldberg's willingness to see Michael again, the producer had another first choice for the part—New York theater actor Matthew Broderick. When Matthew decided against moving to Los Angeles, Michael got a second chance. Matthew went on to star in such films as *Ferris Bueller's Day Off, Election,* and *The Cable Guy.* Michael got to audition again. This time he was perfect. Gary David Goldberg wanted to hire him. Unfortunately, now the executives at NBC were not sure. "Does he have the type of face you'd put on a lunchbox?" one of them asked. In other words, did Michael have the potential to become a break-out star? Was he the type of good-looking guy teenage girls swoon over?

Thinking of Michael's size, Gary David Goldberg said, "Maybe not a lunch box, but at least a thermos."

Michael J. Fox got the job. The role would not only change his bank balance— it would also change his life.

Michael blew his first audition for *Family Ties.*

Chapter 3
Movie Star!

Family Ties was not an immediate hit. In the beginning, it was just another show about a mom and dad and their three kids. There were probably half a dozen other situation comedies—or sitcoms—on TV just like it. Although planned as an ensemble family comedy, just as the "Fonzie" character quickly became the star of *Happy Days*, Michael's "Alex P. Keaton" character became *Family Ties'* star.

The first season it was on the air, the show did not do well in the ratings, but by the end of the year both critics and teen girls had noticed Michael J. Fox. It seemed like the most popular episodes were the ones featuring him. In the second season, his part was emphasized more and the show's ratings improved. By the time the second season ended, *Family Ties* was a top 10 hit.

It was not just the character of Alex P. Keaton who became well known. The actor who played him became a star as well. That first year, remembering his earlier financial problems, Michael was careful with his money. The first car he bought when he was on *Family Ties* was a Honda Prelude. However, soon Michael had all the things big TV stars usually get: a large house, a sports car, and movie offers.

His first project was *Teen Wolf*, a low-budget movie which told the struggle of Michael's character as a high school student coping with becoming a werewolf. Although he found the script funny, even Michael knew it was not the kind of film that would turn him into a star. Michael's first shot at that kind of opportunity arrived almost the same way his first TV break did. Eric Stoltz had starred in the drama *Mask* and was a well-known actor by the time he was hired for the lead role in the science fiction comedy *Back to the*

Remembering his earlier financial problems, Michael was careful with his money.

Future. Unfortunately, Eric was not very funny.

Most movies take approximately three months to film. Eric had worked for nearly five weeks when the producers decided to replace him with another actor. It was an unusual decision and a very expensive one. If they did not find the right actor for the lead role quickly, the movie would never be completed. Michael was fast becoming one of the hottest comedic actors on television. Offering him the job seemed like a natural choice.

> **Michael was fast becoming one of the hottest comedic actors on television.**

There was only one problem. Michael could not take the time off from *Family Ties* in order to make a movie. The young actor found a solution. He would do both. Every day he worked as Alex on *Family Ties* from 10 A.M. to 6 P.M. Each night he was Marty McFly in *Back to the Future.* Most nights he did not finish shooting the movie until 2 A.M.

It was an exhausting schedule, but the hard work paid off. When *Back to the Future* came out in the summer of 1985, it was the number-one movie in the country for weeks. It would go on to earn over $300 million worldwide. By that time, *Family*

Michael in Back to the Future

Ties was the number-two show on TV. Although the low-budget movie *Teen Wolf* was finished filming before *Back to the Future,* it was released to theaters afterwards. Despite its cheap production costs, it went on to earn $40 million — a great deal more than it cost to make.

It was obvious that Michael had the chance to become a movie star. He continued to act on *Family Ties,* reportedly earning over $100,000 an episode by his final show in 1989. His movie career,

When Michael tried to play something different, the audience stayed away.

however, was not as successful. The movie *The Secret of my Success* lived up to its name, but Michael's portrayal of the lead character as an ambitious man trying to get ahead in a large corporation was very similar to his role as Alex Keaton. When he tried to play something different — a soldier in *Casualties of War* or a drug addict in *Bright Lights, Big City* — the audience stayed away. Only *Back to the Future*'s two sequels made a great deal of money. By the early 1990s, Michael J. Fox was not only absent from television, he was also having a difficult time remaining a movie star. It would take an old boss and an American President to give him another chance.

Chapter 4
Back to TV

Although his career was filled with challenges, by the late 1980s Michael J. Fox's personal life was becoming much more stable. He had spent much of the previous 10 years as a successful single actor, dating a variety of actresses, including current *Friends* star Courtney Cox-Arquette and Nancy McKeon from the early '80s TV show, *The Facts of Life*. Nancy appeared with Michael in two made-for-TV movies, *Poison Ivy* and *High School USA.*, while Cox played his girlfriend on several episodes of *Family Ties*.

But it took another actress who played Alex's girlfriend, Tracy Pollan, to change his life.

By the late 1980s Michael's personal life was becoming much more stable.

When Tracy was on *Family Ties*, she and Michael were both in committed relationships with other people. But when she won a supporting role in the film *Bright Lights, Big City* in 1987, the pair quickly fell in love. Shortly after filming was completed, Michael proposed to Tracy.

The two were married in Woodstock, Vermont near where Michael

Michael with his wife Tracy Pollan

had purchased a 120-acre farm he named Lottery Hill. While he continued to work in movie projects including *Greedy* and *The Frighteners*, he tried to spend more and more time with his family. In 1989, he and

Tracy had a son, Sam. Twin daughters Aquinnah and Schuyler were born in 1995.

Upset with the failure of his films to connect with his fans, Michael hired a new agent to get him different roles. In 1994, he was offered a supporting part in *The American President*.

Many movie stars are reluctant to take supporting roles. Although some, like Kevin Bacon in *JFK* and Tom Cruise in *Magnolia*, have done so successfully, many actors worry that taking supporting parts makes them seem smaller. Michael was not concerned. He jumped at the chance to work with actors like Michael Douglas, Martin Sheen, and Annette Bening in director Rob Reiner's film. When *The American President* was released, many felt Michael stole every scene he was in.

The critics and audiences were not the only ones who felt that way. His old boss agreed. *Family Ties* producer Gary David Goldberg had his own share of failed projects after *Family Ties* like *American Dreamer* and *Brooklyn Bridge*. When he saw his old star in *The American President*, he realized the political passion

Upset with the failure of his films to connect with his fans, Michael hired a new agent to get him different roles.

Michael brought to the role could work in a TV series. It gave him a great idea.

Gary David Goldberg told Michael his idea. Michael agreed, but insisted on a few conditions. He wanted to be one of the producers, meaning he would have more say over the scripts, the cast, and other aspects of the show than he had as an actor. The show should be filmed in New York, where he kept an apartment, so he could be home with his family. He also wanted a large, strong cast, so that even if he were the star of the show, the other characters would be very important. To Goldberg the decisions seemed humble, and in part they were. But Michael had another reason.

Just a few years before, Michael J. Fox had learned something that would affect his life forever.

Chapter 5
A New Direction

In many ways, Michael J. Fox has had a great life. He's been a television star and a movie star. He has a successful marriage and healthy children. But in 1991, Michael got some very bad news.

He was in Gainesville, Florida filming the movie *Doc Hollywood* when he noticed his left pinkie finger would sometimes move a little. He did not know why and he realized he could not control it. But he was busy working and decided it was not anything to worry about.

Doc Hollywood was the story of an ambitious young plastic surgeon forced to work as a doctor in a rural town in order to pay off a debt. It was a light comedy— the

Michael was filming a movie when he noticed his left pinkie finger sometimes moved a little.

Michael often speaks to encourage funding for Parkinson's research.

kind Michael's fans seemed to love the most. It did well at the box office, but Michael would not make too many more films like it. Few people knew why his career seemed to fade in the early '90s.

The reason had nothing to do with losing interest in being an actor and everything to do with that strange twitch he had noticed in his pinkie.

In an interview with Oprah Winfrey's *O* Magazine, Michael remembered talking to his wife, "I called her and said, 'Tracy, there's something weird going on with my hand.' She of course said, 'Don't worry, it's nothing.' Then I come home from the doctor [a year later] and say, 'Honey, I have an incurable brain disease - how about that?'"

Doctors had diagnosed Michael with Parkinson's disease. This brain disorder rarely affects people under the age of 50. Michael J. Fox was 30 years old. Parkinson's disease was discovered in the early 1800s by James Parkinson, and it affects about two out of every 1,000 people. It is the result of a lowered level of dopamine in the brain, which influences body movement. It is believed to be a genetic disease, but may also be triggered by the environment. Parkinson's is a degenerative disease. That means its sufferers slowly get worse and worse. There is no cure.

At first, according to Tracy, Michael began to drink more often. He made fewer movies and the ones he did were not very successful. He did some voice-overs — lending his voice to the lead characters in both *Stuart Little* movies, *Homeward Bound*, and *Atlantis: The Lost Empire*. He also directed some television shows, including

Doctors had diagnosed Michael with Parkinson's disease, an incurable brain disease.

an episode of his mentor Gary David Goldberg's program *Brooklyn Bridge*. He tried to continue his life as best as possible.

Still, severe depression is something seen in a number of Parkinson's patients, and Michael was no exception. As a relatively young man with a great career and stable family life, the disease hit him very hard. Only when he got into therapy in 1994 did he slowly learn how to deal with the mental side effects his illness caused.

While it was impossible to become completely physically healthy, becoming mentally healthy had an enormous impact on Michael's career. In the mid-1990s when his old producer Goldberg offered him a chance to be on *Spin City*, Michael was ready for the opportunity.

Premiering in 1996, *Spin City* cast Michael as Michael Flaherty, the deputy mayor of New York City. Filmed in New York, where Michael kept an apartment, he worked hard to have a normal family life. The show itself was successful, both in the ratings and with critics. Michael won three Golden Globes and an Emmy award for his work on *Spin City*.

Michael won three Golden Globes and an Emmy award for his work on *Spin City*.

Although he kept his disease a secret from all but his closest friends, by the late 1990s the tremors that had been under control with medication became more and more noticeable.

Michael with the cast of Spin City

In 1998, he told the public about his condition. The admission did more than let his fans know about what he was dealing with. It also was his first step in working towards finding a cure for the disease. In 2000, he created the Michael J. Fox Foundation for Parkinson's Research, lending his name and considerable resources to his goal: finding a cure within 10 years.

The year 2000 represented another major decision in Michael's life. The stress of being both the star and a producer of *Spin City* eventually became too much. He decided to leave the program, although he planned to still be involved in its production. Actor Charlie Sheen became the show's new deputy mayor and Spin City relocated to Los Angeles, California. It has continued to be successful.

Despite the challenges in his life, Michael does not like to complain. As he put it in his *O Magazine* interview, "What am I going to do with regrets? I only have so much time in the day."

In November 2001 Michael and Tracy had their fourth child, a baby girl named Esme Annabelle Fox.

Michael now uses most of his time to focus on getting funding for his foundation that supports medical research in hopes of finding a cure for Parkinson's disease. He has written an autobiography, the story of his life and work. Published in 2002, the book is entitled, appropriately, *Lucky Man: A Memoir* (Hyperion). His share of the book proceeds will go to his Michael J. Fox Foundation for Parkinson's Research. He is optimistic that his efforts will provide breakthroughs—new medications, improving the quality of life, and hopefully a cure.

> **Despite the challenges in his life, Michael does not like to complain.**

Filmography

Movies

1980 - *Midnight Madness*
1982 - *Class of 1984*
1985 - *Back to the Future*
1985 - *Teen Wolf*
1987 - *Light of Day*
1987 - *The Secret of My Success*
1988 - *Bright Lights, Big City*
1989 - *Casualties of War*
1989 - *Back to the Future II*
1990 - *Back to the Future III*
1991 - *The Hard Way*
1991 - *Doc Hollywood*
1993 - *For Love or Money*
1993 - *Homeward Bound: The Incredible Journey* (voice)
1993 - *Life with Mikey*
1995 - *Blue in the Face*
1995 - *Greedy*
1995 - *The American President*
1996 - *Homeward Bound II: Lost in San Francisco* (voice)
1996 - *The Frighteners*
1996 - *Mars Attacks*
1999 - *Stuart Little* (voice)
2001 - *Atlantis: The Lost Empire* (voice)
2002 - *Stuart Little 2* (voice)
2002 - *Interstate 60*
2002 - *Magic 7* (voice)

Television

1976 - *Leo and Me*
1979 - *Letters from Frank*
1980-1981 - *Palmerstown, USA*
1980 - *Trouble in High Timber Country*
1982-1989 - *Family Ties*
1983 - *High School USA*
1985 - *Poison Ivy*
1987 - *Dear America: Letters Home from Vietnam*
1991 - *Tales from the Crypt: The Trap*
1994 - *Brooklyn Bridge*
1994 - *Don't Drink the Water*
1996-2000 - *Spin City*

Chronology

Index